The Everybody Bicycle

By Joy Cowley

Illustrated by Mike Lacey

Dominie Press, Inc.

Publisher: Christine Yuen
Editor: John S. F. Graham
Designer: Lois Stanfield
Illustrator: Mike Lacey

Published by:

🐪 **Dominie Press, Inc.**

1949 Kellogg Avenue
Carlsbad, California 92008 USA

www.dominie.com

Paperback ISBN 0-7685-1076-7
Library Bound Edition ISBN 0-7685-1525-4
Printed in Singapore by PH Productions Pte Ltd
   3 4 5 6 PH 04 03

Table of Contents

Chapter One

Fresh Bread

Many years ago,
in a small town,
there was a boy called Tom,
who wanted to work for a baker
before school each morning.

"I need someone to deliver bread,"
the baker said to Tom.
"I've got customers all over town
who expect fresh bread and buns
before breakfast. This means
you must pedal fast on your bicycle."

"I don't have a bicycle," said Tom.

"Then get one," said the baker.
"No bicycle—no job."

Tom went home
and said to his brother Abe,
"How can I get a bicycle
when I don't have any money?"

Abe laughed. "Make one," he said.

"Ha-ha, very funny," said Tom.

Chapter Two

Could He Really Do That?

Tom wanted a bicycle
more than anything in the world.
He had no money to buy one,
but he remembered Abe's words.

Could he make a bicycle?
Could he really do that?

He had seen an old frame
lying at the edge of the river.
It had nothing on it—
no wheels, no handlebars,
no pedals, and no seat.

He went to the river
and pulled the bicycle frame
out of the mud.
It was rusty in parts
and dripping with wet weeds.

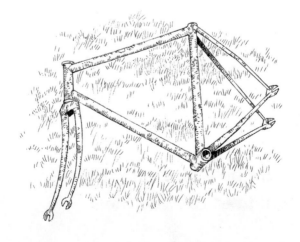

"Trash!" said Abe.

"You can't do anything with that!"

Tom stared at the muddy frame.

"I'm going to try," he replied.

Chapter Three
Just What I Need

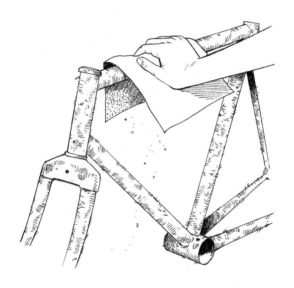

Under the mud and rust,
the bicycle frame was still strong.
Tom rubbed it with sandpaper.

He said to Abe,
"Now I am going to ask people
if they have any bicycle parts
they don't want."

"You're really going to try
and make a bicycle?" said Abe.

"I sure am," Tom said.

He went to the house next door
where Mrs. Norman lived.
No, she didn't have any bicycle
parts, but she gave him some cake
with lemon frosting.
"Making a bicycle is hungry work,"
she told him.

"Thank you," Tom said.

Auntie Louise,
who lived across the road,
had two bicycle wheels
hanging on the wall in her shed.
They were different sizes,
but they were strong wheels.

"Perfect!" Tom said.

Mr. Karabo, down the road,
had a bicycle chain
and a box of nuts and bolts.
"Help yourself," he said to Tom.
"I'm glad someone can
make use of them."

"These will do great!" Tom said.

Mr. Laterre, who sold fish,
knew where there was
a set of handlebars.
"I saw it in the trash," he said,
"and I told myself
that it might be handy one day,
so I put it in my basement."

"Handlebars!" cried Tom.
"Just what I need!"

Chapter Four

Tires and Inner Tubes

Word swept around the town.
The boy who wanted
to work for the baker
was building a bicycle.
He needed parts.

People knocked on Tom's door.
They left boxes on the front porch.

By the middle of the week,
Tom had everything
except the tires and inner tubes.

He knew he could not use
old tires and inner tubes.
How could he get new ones?

Mr. Green at the gas station
repaired bicycle tires
as well as car tires.

He said to Tom,
"If you clean my garage,
I'll give you some tires
and inner tubes."

Tom worked for three days,
sweeping the gas station,
tidying the benches,
and scrubbing oil off the floor.

Mr. Green was pleased.

"Here, Tom," he said.

"These tires and inner tubes are new.

And they're different sizes

to fit your different-sized wheels."

"Thank you!" cried Tom.

Now that he had everything he needed,
Tom would be able to start working
at the bakery next Monday morning!

He walked home, whistling,
the tires and inner tubes
under his arm.

Abe was waiting for him
with a can of bright red paint.
"This is for the everybody bicycle,"
said Abe.
"People will see you coming."

Tom laughed. "Thanks, Abe.
The everybody bicycle
is going to look like a fire engine."

"With bread instead of hoses,"
said Abe.

Chapter Five

A New Bicycle

The bright red everybody bicycle
did look a bit odd,
but it went very fast.
Every morning,
Tom whizzed around town,
delivering bread and buns.

People smiled and waved
as the boy sped past them.
"Nice chain you've got there!"
called Mr. Karabo.

"Funny looking wheels!"
chuckled Auntie Louise.
"Where'd you get those crazy things?"

Tom waved back,
in too much of a hurry to reply.

He worked so hard
that at the end of the year
he had earned enough money
to buy a new bicycle.
But he did not ride the new bicycle.
He gave it to his brother Abe,
and they worked together,
delivering bread and buns.

Sometimes, after school,
they worked in the bakery.
The baker showed them
how to make good bread dough.
He also showed them
how to make dough for pizza.

Chapter Six

Pizza Shops

When the brothers grew up,
they started a pizza shop
in the next town.
They hired boys with bicycles
to do the deliveries.

One pizza shop became two.
Two pizza shops became four.

Now Tom and Abe
have pizza shops
all across the country.

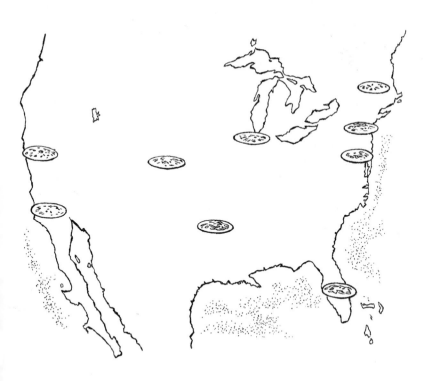

On the wall in Tom's office
hangs the old red-painted bicycle
with the different-sized wheels.

When people visit Tom's office,
he points to the old bicycle.
"This is my everybody bicycle,"
he tells the visitors.
"The people in my town
gave me the parts to build it.
That's how I got started,
and that's why I call our business,

The Everybody Pizza Company!"